By: Allen Paul Weaver III

Copyright © 2013 by Allen Paul Weaver III

All rights reserved. No part of this publication may be reproduced, stored in a retrieval system, or transmitted in any form or by any means—electronic, mechanical, photocopy, recording, or otherwise—except for brief quotations in printed reviews, without the prior written permission of the author.

'Unknown Fear' is written by Allen Paul Weaver III and is from, Transition: Breaking Through the Barriers, Pg. 101. Published by: IUniverse June 2006

Multiple Intelligence Theory listing excerpt is from:
The MI Strategy Bank, by Dr. Ellen Arnold
Used with permission.

Cover and interior design: Robert Giorgio.

All Scripture is quoted from the King James Bible.

Published by: Radiant City Studios, LLC

Books may be ordered by contacting:
Allen Paul Weaver III at **www.allenpaulweaveriii.com**

ISBN: 978-0-9961045-1-7 (pbk)

Printed in the United States of America

DEDICATION

This book is dedicated to YOU the reader: to who you've been, who you are and who you will become. Allow this book to help you learn from your past, inform your present, and prepare for your future. Let this book help you dream. Use this book as fuel to propel you forward! As much as you are waiting on destiny... Destiny is waiting on you.

NOTE TO READERS

This publication contains the opinions and ideas of its author. It is intended to provide helpful and informative material on the subjects addressed. The strategies outlined in this book may not be suitable for every individual, and are not guaranteed or warranted to produce any particular results.

This book is sold with the understanding that the author is not engaged in rendering legal, financial, accounting, or other professional advice or services. The reader should consult a competent professional before adopting any of the suggestions in this book or drawing inferences from it.

No warranty is made with respect to the accuracy or completeness of the information or references contained herein, and the author specifically disclaims any responsibility for any liability, loss or risk, personal or otherwise, which is incurred as a consequence, directly or indirectly, of the use and application of any of the contents of this book.

TABLE OF CONTENTS

INTRODUCTION

MOVE MANIFESTO

PROLOGUE:
A Reluctant Dreamer

CHAPTER 1
Standing Still Could Get You Killed!

CHAPTER 2
Success Without Significance?

CHAPTER 3
Questions Don't Matter Unless…

CHAPTER 4
Hiding In Plain Sight!

CHAPTER 5
Overcoming Obstacles

CHAPTER 6
Moving Forward

Allen's Reading List
Books to Help You 'MOVE!'

Acknowledgements

About the Author

Did You Like This Book?

Have Allen to Speak at Your Next Event

INTRODUCTION

THERE ARE A NUMBER OF STORIES IN THE BIBLE THAT AMAZE ME. Two such passages are when God calls Abram (soon to be known as Abraham), and later his descendants—the Hebrew people—to journey to a place they've never known: the Promise Land. Just read the accounts beginning in Genesis 12 and in Exodus 3. What amazes me is this: <u>God had a dream for them; but they had to be willing to MOVE.</u>

They had an idea about what their life and destiny would be—which was based on the reality of their current living conditions. However, God had an entirely different dream for them! As they moved, they did face obstacles and difficulties... but these challenges didn't negate the fact that a destination was waiting for them. Sadly, there were some who didn't reach the Promise Land—not because it wasn't available—but because they allowed fear and unbelief to cloud their judgment, and by extension, their actions. Their destiny was waiting for them... but they had disqualified themselves.

I want you to do this exercise: imagine that you are a yellow number two pencil lying on a table... Its potential is locked up inside of it, but that pencil will lie there indefinitely unless moved by an outside force. Its destiny seems set. But what happens if someone walks by and picks up the pencil? The possibilities become endless! Scribbles form words, which are strung together to warm a person's heart. Contrasts between shapes and shades unify to create artwork that captures the eyes. Dark and light circles combine with lines and dashes, to form the foundation for music that is sweet to the ears. Numbers line up to form equations that unlock the mysteries of the world around us. Designs are forged. Ideas are fleshed with clarity. Dreams come to pass. Destiny is realized. All because the pencil was not allowed to merely remain on the table alone... but was put into motion.

I can't make you MOVE in life. That decision is up to you. But I can provide concepts, life experiences and perspectives that can:

A. Help you understand the type of struggles you will face when you MOVE.

B. Reveal ways to overcome these obstacles.

C. Transform your ability to evaluate decisions in light of your available options.

As much as you are waiting on destiny, even more so, your destiny is waiting on you. That means you have to get up and do something new. My hope is that wherever you MOVE, whatever you choose to pursue and explore, it will be a direction that develops you as a person so you can positively impact others.

MOVING BUSINESS

I discovered, at the beginning of 2013, that I'm in the moving business. Basically, all of my adult life has essentially been about helping others move from where they are to where they need and want to be. When I talk with people about pursuing the deep dreams that live in their hearts, one question comes up repeatedly: "Allen, how do I MOVE?" Often, behind that question lies a fear. More than any other reason for our lack of action is fear: fear of failure, fear of rejection, fear of... You fill in the blank. And most of the time it is that fear which keeps us from moving forward to capitalize on the opportunities that are in front of us.

Have you ever had to move from one city to another? It can be a scary time because you have to leave everything behind that's familiar to you: your home, your friends, your routine. You leave all of those things behind to go to a place you have never been before—hoping that new opportunities will lead to a life of greater fulfillment.

When I was a little boy my family moved from Florida to New York. It was a scary time for me. I didn't want to leave! Everything I had known, understood and relied upon was in Florida! All my friends and favorite places to go were in Florida! I knew nothing about New York. I can remember crying as I hugged my two closest friends, Carlos and Erica. I also remember the group of people who gathered to see us off. Their smiles seemed forced... Their hugs were long and tight.

I never thought I'd have to move. I loved everything about where I already was! But my dad had a clear destination in mind for us. It was new. It was unknown. And ... it was full of possibilities and opportunities. So, we prepared the best we could for the move and took the plunge.

We threw out all of our junk. With help from others, we packed up our possessions and put it on the truck. Then we took the long drive from Florida to New York while making stops along the way. And once we arrived, others helped us move into our new home. Then the process of getting used to our new life began. Years later, my family can look back and say that this was a good MOVE!

If you want to live a life of greater success and significance, you will have to be willing to MOVE from where you are to where you need and want to be.

LEVELED SUCCESS

At some level every person on the planet is successful – and that includes you. Maybe you learned how to tie your shoelaces or to tell time or to count to ten. Congratulations! You are successful! Now, you probably think this is trivial (and in a way it is), but the truth is that daily, most of us believe we are unsuccessful in our lives. Day-by-day many of us beat ourselves up over our failures – what we are unable to accomplish. Our own internal speech says something like, "I am such a failure. I will never be successful. I will never be able to overcome my struggles. I wish I were never born. Things will never change."

We spend an extremely huge amount of time and mental energy focusing on what we have yet to "get right" in life. Our focus on the negative is so consuming that we often define our existence and our worth by our lack. But let me ask you a few questions. What is going right in your life? What have you been successful at doing? What do you like about your life? Take a few moments to write down your answers to these questions.

You are successful – even if it's only at small levels. Don't forget, small things add up to support and create big endeavors. Imagine getting dressed in the morning and forgetting how to button your pants; or purchasing something from the store and not being able to count your money. What if you had to head to the airport to catch a plane and you didn't know how to tell time?

So, don't discount your small successes. Let them add up over time every day. Your goal is to determine how to take your small, daily successes and translate them into larger life successes that enable you to MOVE from where you are to where you need and want to be! And this book was written to help you do just that. This process begins with gaining a new perspective.

WHAT ARE YOU BUILDING?

Whether we know it or not - we are ALL building our lives. Right now, our past and present decisions are determining what type of future we will most likely experience. Some of you are well on your way to building a significant life. Some of you don't care about what type of life you are building. Some of you do care, but don't know the necessary steps for building a successful life.

My desire is for you to be in a better place when you leave than when you came in. If you have no plan - let's get you a plan. If you already have a plan - let's get you more clarity. In order to do that, we need to take some time to ask some key questions.

Those who take the time to stop and consider their lives are the ones who have a higher chance of making something significant out of their lives. And while having knowledge is a major key to success in life, an even bigger key is actually applying the knowledge we have to our circumstances! The world is full of people who have knowledge but don't apply it. This non-application leads to the inability to capitalize on opportunities when they arise.

Hosea 4:6 states *"My people are destroyed for a lack of knowledge…"*

IN THIS BOOK

So, welcome to MOVE! You will find facts, figures, quotes and stories to help you in your journey. At the end of each chapter you will find: **"Moving Tips!"** and **"Get Moving!"** These two sections are designed to provide key points and questions to motivate you forward!

It is my hope and prayer that the content within these pages will help enable you to MOVE from where you are to where you need and want to be.

MOVING TIPS!

Don't discount your small successes. Let them add up over time every day. Your goal is to determine how to take your small, daily successes and translate them into larger life-successes that enable you to MOVE from where you are to where you need and want to be!

If you want to live a life of greater success and significance, you must be willing to MOVE from where you are to where you need and want to be.

GET MOVING!

Here are questions that can help you move forward.

A. In what areas of your life have you been successful?

B. In what areas of your life have you been unsuccessful?

MOVE MANIFESTO

A PERSONAL DECLARATION:

"In order for me to MOVE, I must have MOTIVATION: a reason to take the first step forward and every step thereafter. In order for me to MOVE, I need OPTIMISM: an "It's Possible" mindset—otherwise I might as well stay where I am. In order for me to MOVE, I need VISION: the ability to see opportunities in the midst of challenges and difficulties. In order for me to MOVE, I must have ENTHUSIASM: a passion for my journey that beckons others to MOVE in their own lives as well."

TEN ESSENTIAL TRUTHS

1. **Everyone is important.** But each of us must become significant.
2. **We are born** with talents that must be discovered, developed and displayed.
3. **Through circumstance** we inherit baggage, which must be unpacked, understood and overcome if we are to truly contribute to the betterment of society.
4. **Each of us** has a skill-SET: a unique way we demonstrate our life story, experiences and talents. We must learn what our skill-SET is and how to put it to work to help us excel in life.
5. **Daily exercising our** body, mind and spirit is key to fully carrying out our life's purpose.
6. **Harboring an unhealthy** sense of fear leads to our lack of purpose and fulfillment.
7. **We navigate the world** through questions. Therefore we must always have a mindset to keep asking questions.
8. **Failure is only** failure if we don't learn from it.
9. **Significance comes by** pursuing God's Dream for our life, while helping others along the way.
10. **There is a** time to stand still… and there is a time to MOVE! We must learn the difference and act accordingly.

Allen Paul Weaver III, 2013

PROLOGUE:
A Reluctant Dreamer

I WASN'T SUPPOSED TO BE HERE. That's the thought that runs through my head as my two-and-a-half year old son asks, "Daddy do you want to play with me?" The reality that I am living a future I couldn't even imagine tumbles around in my mind - like wet clothes in a hot dryer.

One of my greatest victories was overcoming low self-esteem - which led to my suicide attempt back in 1992. It was a month before my eighteenth birthday and after I was already accepted to college. Years worth of negative thinking about my self-worth had come to a boil: the color of my skin, my glasses, the high pitch of my voice, my sweaty palms and feet, my skinny physique (like "Roger" from the television show, "What's Happening"). Some of my peers would make fun of me, but I learned to laugh in order to mask the pain.

Adults would often tell me, "Allen, you're going to be somebody when you grow up." But the future seemed so far away... so unattainable. No, there was no future for me. I was stuck. And my circumstances would never change. The only way to make the pain stop was to cease living. But my suicide attempt failed - not due to my negligence - but due to an intervention by God. The next day, my feet stood at the very spot where I desperately waited for death to come for me. My eyes looked toward the blue sky and I said, "Lord, you didn't let me die last night. So, you must have a purpose for me. I don't know what it is... but I want it."

I'd like to say that after that moment in my life everything instantly got better! But that was not the case. The process of daily walking out truth began - the Bible calls it "renewing your mind" - and what a hard process it was! An incessant replacing of negative thoughts with positive ones! Making an attempt to believe what I'd never known to be true for me. And I think part of the reason it was so hard was because I was afraid to dream of a bright future for myself. Helping others dream for themselves? Check! Dreaming for myself? Mmmm... Not quite. Somehow, my subconscious routinely whispered that I wasn't worthy of a good life. It was a nagging feeling in the back of my mind that I couldn't shake. But, God has been slowly teaching me how to dream by using his track record of intervention in my life in conjunction with his word.

"Now unto him that is able to do exceeding abundantly above all that we ask or think, according to the power that worketh in us..."
(Ephesians 3:20)

Over time, I began having small dreams. And as God brought them to pass, my ability to imagine a life for myself grew. Here's some of the track record so far:

Delivered from low self-esteem and suicidal thoughts. Graduated from college and graduate school. Worked for several great organizations, including Walt Disney World Inc., and Universal Studios Florida. Traveled across the United States and to seven African countries, Europe, China, the Bahamas and Aruba. Author of two published books. Independent film producer. Artist. Composer. Teacher. Mentor. Public speaker. Preacher. Son. Brother. Friend. Husband. Father.

When I was about to turn 30, I had a mid-life crisis. The question that played over and over in my mind was, "What have I done with my life?" My twenties were coming to an end, and from where I was standing; the answers I focused on weren't very encouraging. However, it was the responses of family and friends who helped me to put my life in perspective. They helped me to focus - not only on my weaknesses and failures - but also on my accomplishments and my ability to help others accomplish their dreams.

Sure, my life wasn't perfect: obstacles waited to be conquered and endeavors remained to be pursued. But I was a long way from insignificance... And it was this revelation that began to change my perspective on life.

So here I am, less than two years from forty and the life I've had - while not perfect - has been beyond my imagination! So, when I hold my son in my arms and he laughs, or gives me a hug, or is sleeping, or tells me he loves me, or even cries... I try to remind myself that: for all of the negatives in my life; all of my past and present failures; all of the things that didn't go according to plan; all of my financial woes; and all of my "woulda-coulda-shouldas"... There are many things that are going right. And now I see with greater clarity, the necessity of having a plan for my life. For the times that I had one, my ability to take advantage of opportunities was greater.

"Commit thy works unto the LORD, and thy thoughts shall be established." (Proverbs 16:3)

I continue to learn that God is in the business of creating dreams. And he has given us the task of chasing after them. And it is in the pursuit that we discover who we are and who we were created to become.

What he has given me is the desire to help you discover, pursue and walk out his dream for your life. It's time to move from where you are to where you need and want to be.

CHAPTER 1: Standing Still Could Get You Killed!

SO THERE I WAS... A MIDDLE SCHOOL STUDENT CAUGHT IN THE SIGHTS OF A BARKING, GROWLING, RAZOR-TEETH BEARING GERMAN SHEPHERD! The neighborhood dog that nobody liked (and who didn't like anybody) had broken loose and was barreling up the residential street towards me! I was walking to church, while wearing a white dress shirt, black slacks and penny loafers with the slippery soles. Immediately I knew I couldn't outrun the large, angry dog. There was no safe place to go and there was no one around to help! Standing still would mean certain death - or at least a sure maiming. I had to move somewhere, and in that desperate moment, an idea entered my mind.

Suddenly I started moving as fast as I could - not away from the dog - but towards it! I ran at that dog and started yelling at the top of my lungs, "Come on!!!" If I was going down, it wouldn't be without a fight! An amazing thing happened as I charged at the dog. The dog screeched to a halt turned around and took off in the other direction! Now I was chasing it up the street yelling, "Get back here!!!"

After a moment, my pace slowed as the dog ran back into its yard. A moment later I turned and headed to church - blown away by what had just happened. And I never had another problem with that dog again.

Now, I'm not saying that you should chase dogs up the street, but there are times when you have to move. There are times when standing still will get you killed. There are times when retreat is not an option. And you have to be able to understand those times and act accordingly. To misinterpret those times will mean a loss of growth opportunities and chances to impact others.

Now is the time for us to MOVE from where we are to where we need and want to be. Now is the time to MOVE towards a life of greater success and significance. Now is the time to MOVE beyond our areas of struggle. Why? Because we will never know who we truly are and what we are fully capable of if we don't. Don't you want to know what it's like to live an abundant life? To be free from internal anxiety? To operate at your peak efficiency mentally, physically, emotionally, spiritually and financially? To be fully alive, fully creative, fully compassionate, fully loving, fully present in the moment and fully able to see the truth that's right in front of you and act accordingly? What would it be like to live a life where you conquered every negative limitation?

There is a reason that in every generation the masses are exposed to those few individuals who seem to break through every conventional barrier and accomplish what is seemingly impossible. Here are just a few examples of such individuals:

Plato. Socrates. Beethoven. Bach. Michelangelo. Leonardo Davinci. Mozart. Shakespeare. Benjamin Banneker. George Washington Carver. The Wright Brothers. Walt Disney. Einstein. Gandhi. Martin Luther King, Jr. John F. Kennedy. Mother Theresa. Michael Jordan. Dr. Randy Pausch. Bill Gates. Steve Jobs.

These individuals serve as object lesson reminders to us - letting is know that we too can be free... if we are willing to take the journey.

Now is the time for us to MOVE to a life of greater success and significance. Why? Because when we live fully we inspire others! People are waiting on us: People who are struggling and wondering how they are going to make it! People who are afraid to dream of a better life. People who are being chased and bullied by negative situations - who feel stuck and cornered. Even people who are trying to pursue their dreams! They all need to hear our stories of struggle, perseverance and triumph! They need to know that "better" is possible. They need to see for themselves - through us - that they can MOVE.

History is full of people who chose to MOVE! This idea and concept didn't start with us, but it can continue through us. You and I can MOVE. But, let me tell you... This won't be easy. But it's not impossible.

You moving towards your God-given purpose will require willingness, discipline and focus. It will also require imagination, creativity and vision casting. This will be tough; but so is exercise. But just like exercise, if you consistently do it the right way, you will find yourself growing stronger and looking better over time! Are you ready to MOVE? Then let's go!

A MOVING BLUEPRINT

Life Point: Anything built must first begin with a blueprint.

Every created object you see, hear, taste, touch and smell all started with a blueprint. From the chair you're sitting on, to the vehicles you ride in, someone got an idea for the object and had it designed on paper before it was built. Based on its design and purpose - steps were taken to build the object. If obstacles were encountered, alternatives and adaptations were created by focusing on the object's purpose and by using solution-based thinking.

We can understand this process when it comes to creating objects, but many of us don't realize that this truth also applies to our human lives. We too are building something. It is our life: an object of great worth. And in the process of building our lives we are also developing our soul. But many of us wander through life with no blueprint, no game plan, no real idea about where we came from and where we're going. And so we build our lives - mostly haphazardly - using whatever materials we find along the way. In a sense, we mix precious metals with cheap substitutes and fillers, and then wonder why our lives fall apart. In some ways, it's like our true intent is to tear down our life - like a wrecking ball demolishes a condemned building.

Anything built must first begin with a blueprint. Do you have a blueprint for your life? If you don't have one, do you want a blueprint for your life? If your answer is yes to either of these questions, then keep reading.

DO YOU WANT TO BE A "FAILURENAIRE?"

I have yet to meet someone whose life-long dream was to grow up to be unsuccessful. However, I have met people who didn't know their purpose, were unsure of their abilities, were afraid to take advantage of opportunities, and were uncertain about their future.

The closest I've come was years ago when I met a sixteen year old on his birthday. I asked what he wanted to be when he grew up. His response still unnerves me today. He looked me in the eye and without hesitation said, "I don't think I'm gonna be anything." Due to my shock, I had no response for him. What kind of pressure was he experiencing that, on what should have been a day of celebration, he had no hope for the future? He wasn't saying, "I want to be unsuccessful." In fact, he was saying, "I don't see how I can be successful."

And it is this lack of "seeing" that is crippling to us. Helen Keller once said, "The only thing worse than being blind is having sight but no vision." The truth is that many of our youth grow up and become unsuccessful. And many adults are filled with fears, doubts. Both groups face unsuccessful situations. Why? While external factors may play a role in their predicament, the greater controlling factor is their ability to see (or lack thereof) that affects the decisions they make about the choices that are presented to them. If you want to have a new outcome in your life, you will most likely have to make new decisions. To make new decisions, you have to begin to see things differently. Once you can see differently, then you can begin to make a series of small steps towards your goals. Dr. R. Lamar Vest, former president and CEO of American Bible Society, coined a term for this series of small steps: "Relentless Incrementalism."

What do you see? What kind of decisions are you making about the choices presented in life? Where are your decisions taking you? Even if you can't see the "Big Picture," take some time to plot out the direction you would like to go. Then you will be able to start taking small steps towards your goal. As I stated earlier in a slightly different way, "small successes over time build up to larger opportunities." Now is the time to decide that you want to make better decisions. *N.O.W. - No Opportunity Wasted.* This is your opportunity.

THE RIGHT QUESTIONS

Did you answer, "No" to the question, "Do you want to be a failure in life?" If you don't want to be a failure, then you have to start asking new questions about the life you desire to live. Then you must be intentional about pursuing the answers to the questions.

In the Bible, God states, *"I call heaven and earth to record this day against you, that I have set before you life and death, blessing and cursing: therefore choose life, that both thou and thy seed may live."* (Deuteronomy 30:19)

It's time to begin asking the right questions about what kind of life you want to live.

Based on God's words above, we see that life is like a multiple-choice test. The great thing about a multiple-choice test is that the right answer is in front of you. The tough thing about a multiple-choice test is that the wrong answer is in front of you as well. The benefit of a multiple-choice test is that the pressure of not knowing the right answer is somewhat alleviated. You have a 50/50 chance of guessing the right answer. You can also use the process of elimination to help you make an educated guess. But if you have absolutely no idea about the subject matter of the test, it is practically impossible to pass on guessing alone.

When presented with a choice - life and death, blessing and cursing are always present. So, if life presents us with opportunities to succeed and fail, the difference will come from our ability to focus on the right things. And we cannot focus on the right things if we are not asking the right questions. Take a moment to answer the questions that are below. Remember... anything built must first begin with a blueprint.

What kind of life do you want? What kind of person do you want to be? What kind of person does God want you to be?

MOVING TIPS!

- Anything built must first begin with a blueprint.

- The greatest controlling factor between success and failure in life are the decisions we make when presented with a myriad of choices over a lifetime.

- If you want to have a new outcome you will have to make new decisions.

- Asking new questions about the life you want decreases the chance of failure.

- Often our lack of success is because we can't SEE how to reach our goals.

GET MOVING!

Here are questions and key thoughts that can help you move forward.

A. Where are you standing still or retreating in your life?

B. Which is better: using a blueprint for your life or 'going with the flow?'

C. How does a lack of "seeing" cripple you?

D. How can you use "Relentless Incrementalism" to help reach your goals?

E. What steps are you currently taking to build your life?

F. Where do you want to be a 1-5 years from now?

CHAPTER 2: Success Without Significance?

"We often judge on the scale of success, what should be measured on the scale of significance."
— Allen Paul Weaver III

MY UNCLE CHARLES...

My uncle, the Rev. Dr. Charles Austin Thurman was born in 1947 and died in 2012. After God, family and ministry, the very next thing my uncle loved was major league baseball. That was his dream as a boy, and he pursued it too. By the time he was ready for college, he had made a name for himself and scouts were already looking at him. His dream seemed in sight... and then God came along and called my uncle into the ministry. He was faced with a dilemma. Would he choose his own dream or the dream that God had for him? He chose to follow hard after God's purpose for his life.

My uncle was a great man. Sadly, I did not realize the full value of this truth until after he died. While he was alive, I knew him as a good man with some measure of success: Outside of being a great husband, father and uncle, he was an educator, a marriage counselor, and an acting dean for Black Church Studies at the very seminary I had attended. But if I am to be honest, from my perspective there were a couple of areas where he seemed unsuccessful. He pastored a church for over thirty years with a membership that never grew beyond the small building. He also worked for a number of years on several book manuscripts, without ever seeing one of them published.

But the uncle I knew always had a knack for encouragement. As a teen, my grandparents would give me, my brother and our two cousins, money for A's. I always received the least amount of money because my A's were typically in physical education, art and chorale. My brother and two cousins would almost break the bank by getting A's in almost every class. But my uncle would always encourage me and say, "Allen, I see you shining in college." And that is exactly what happened.

When I got to college, something just "clicked" and the desire to excel began to burn within me. My college career was one of honor rolls and dean's lists. My graduation was Magna Cum Laude - high honors. After graduation, my uncle smiled and said, "I told you I saw you shining in college." I was amazed that he saw in me what I could not see in myself. Yet, down through the years, I viewed my uncle as a partial success story.

A LESSON FROM DEATH

When my uncle died a couple of days after Christmas 2012, I began to learn an entirely new lesson. Over 400 people came to his home-going celebration! Many drove and flew in from all over the country - braving snowstorms and blizzards to make sure they paid their respects. The funeral lasted over 3 hours, and during that time I received a lesson about the difference between success and significance. So many people talked about how God had used my uncle to impact and change their lives. Young people as well as adults cried and paid tribute to his life and legacy in magnificent ways.

I thought I knew my uncle, but it was at his funeral that I truly realized the significance of his life. It was during this time of mourning that I discovered that while success and significance are related - they are not synonymous.

Success and Significance are not the same. Success is defined as: *The accomplishment of an aim or purpose; the attainment of popularity or profit. Significance is defined as: The quality of being worthy of attention; importance.* Success is about getting things done. Significance is about making a lasting impact and impression on others. Many people are neither successful nor significant. Others are merely successful. Few are both successful and significant.

We often judge things on the scale of success, when it is the scale of significance that is required. To be significant in life is ultimately the true measure of success.

My uncle was the kind of person who acted like you were the only one in the room when you talked with him. He would speak the truth in love – even if the truth wasn't popular. If he felt it could help you – he would say it. He was always concerned about the lives of others - both eternally and in the here-and-now.

The last time I saw my uncle alive was two months before his death - at his youngest daughter's wedding. The last thing he told me was, "pursue the dreams God has placed in your heart. And don't be afraid to ask for help along the way because no one can do everything by themselves."

To develop a true blueprint for life, we must be sure that our plan includes not only success, but also significance. We must also realize that God may have plans for us, which supersede our own, and then be willing to go wherever he wants to lead us.

MID-LIFE CRISIS!

This was a recent lesson about the difference between success and significance. An earlier lesson came when I was twenty-nine. Months from my thirtieth birthday, I found myself in a crisis: a mid-life crisis. "What had I done with my life?" was the repeating question in my mind. And all I could focus on was what was not done.

You see, some of my friends from college had made a pact: we would take the world by storm by the time we were twenty-five. We would be financially independent, successful in our business pursuits and active in giving back to our community and our college alma mater. But here I was, not financially independent, not fully successful in my business pursuits, and not able to give back financially to my community and college. I was living paycheck-to-paycheck and had a lot of credit card debt. And so, I found myself questioning the significance of my existence.

It took a lot of prayer, Bible reading and talking with trusted friends to help me break through my crisis mode. And it was here I learned that while my life's endeavors may not have been completely successful, they were in many ways significant. Many parents shared how my constant interaction with their children had made a difference in their lives. Family and friends shared how my life and the willingness to travel to West Africa to do humanitarian aid work had inspired them to press forward with their own dreams. And my wife listed accomplishments I had lost sight of while focusing on what had not been done.

Encouragement also came from Scripture, when a friend pointed out two facts: 1) Jesus started his public ministry at thirty. 2) Joseph (who was sold into Egyptian slavery by his brothers) was made second-in-command of the entire nation... when he was thirty.

My world didn't have to end at thirty! It was a new decade to transition into greater and more significant things. Here it is over eight years later and my significance and success continues to mature! Now I am close to forty years old and looking forward to what's on the horizon! I am in pursuit of significance, knowing that if my existence can positively impact others for the sake of their purpose, then success won't be far behind. And while in my pursuit, I am working to bring all areas of my life (spiritually, mentally, physically, socially, financially) into proper balance.

MOVING TIPS!

- We often judge on the scale of success, what should be measured on the scale of significance.
- While success and significance are related - they are not synonymous.
- We must be sure that our blueprint includes success and significance.
- Pursue significance and success won't be far behind.

GET MOVING!

Here are questions and key thoughts that can help you move forward.

A. Who speaks positive things into your life? Who do you listen to?

B. What key points/lessons have you received from them?

CHAPTER 3:
Questions Don't Matter Unless...

Life Point: We navigate the world by asking questions.

(This chapter is the "Meat and Potatoes" of the entire book.)

TO THE PERSON WHO ISN'T LOOKING FOR ANSWERS—QUESTIONS DON'T MATTER. To the person who is content with staying at the level they are at, questions that challenge complacency and promote growth don't even enter their mind. Where are you today? I imagine if you are reading these words then questions do matter to you. If I'm honest with you, and myself then I have to admit on the surface, my previous statement about "questions don't matter" is incomplete.

In reality EVERYONE—even those not looking for answers—navigates the world through questions! The distinction is that those not looking for genuine life-changing answers only ask questions that are related to existence: "What time is it?" "What's for dinner?" "What clothes am I going to wear?" And those who want to go someplace in life ask questions that speak to issues of becoming: "Where are you going?" "How do I get there from here?" "How can I make the most out of what I have?" "How can I help you get to your destination?"

Questions are a key component for attaining understanding. Questions help us make sense of our experiences. Questions can also unlock opportunities. Science, technology, medicine, literature, philosophy, theology, psychology, visual arts, civil rights, aviation, education, athletics, exploration, architecture, music, agriculture—all of humanity's greatest achievements have come from questions that were asked. And many of our greatest failures have come from our failure to ask the right questions.

Asking questions makes us vulnerable. It reveals to others that there is something we don't know or understand. And in our information age, people don't like to appear as if they don't understand something. This may be one reason why when an opportunity comes to ask questions while in a group - no one wants to go first. Yet asking questions also reveals a sense of power. It shows that we are courageous enough to seek out answers.

Getting appropriate answers to our questions is another key to attaining understanding, because the more we understand, the better we can act. (Although, having more information doesn't mean we will act on what we know.) Even so, the less we understand, the more fear and ignorance restrict our ability to better ourselves. So, we must wrestle with questions.

Simply stated, "asking the right questions is a key to success! Asking the wrong questions is a key to failure." Asking the right questions opens our eyes to options and leads us down a path to opportunity. Asking the wrong questions blinds us to the possibilities that are right in front of us.

Just think about this example: You are a student sitting in a classroom full of other students. The teacher has been lecturing for almost an hour. You find yourself looking at your watch. Then you ask yourself, "When is this class going to be over?" By doing this, you allow yourself to mentally shut down and completely disregard any helpful information that may be presented. This is asking the wrong question. However, the right question to ask would be, "What helpful information can I take away from this class?" By doing this, you are mentally opening yourself up to seeing new connections, which could lead to new, viable opportunities!

In our busy, distracted society, asking the right questions will mean the difference between failure and success, mediocrity and excellence.

KEEP ASKING QUESTIONS!

In college, my communications department held a panel discussion so students could meet professionals from television, radio and publishing.

The publishing professional was a new author by the name of Omar Tyree. He was a relatively unknown author, but something about his presentation impacted me tremendously. The more he talked, the more questions swelled up within me! When the time came to ask questions, for me it was as if Omar Tyree was the only panelist. Question after question erupted from my mouth. After a while my friends told me to "Shut up." But there was this burning desire within me that had to be satiated. I had to know how he accomplished becoming an author!

After the event, when I spoke to the author personally, he instantly remembered me. "You're the brother who was asking me all of those questions." He gave me a copy of his book and wrote on the inside page: *"To Allen. Keep asking questions!"* This moment helped to change my life forever! It was a few weeks later that I received inspiration to write my first book. And so far, I've published two books and am working on several other manuscripts.

Even though I love to write, I never saw myself as a published author - until meeting (the now notable) Omar Tyree. God used that situation to cause me to dream of a future that I didn't know was possible for me - all through the process of asking questions. We navigate the world by asking questions.

FOUR BIG QUESTIONS TO ASK YOURSELF

1. WHAT IS GOD'S DREAM FOR MY LIFE?

It is my belief that life on earth is not a cosmic accident, but rather a deliberate intention by an all-knowing, all-powerful multi-dimensional Being - the God of the universe. And if God has taken the time to create us, then there must be a purpose for us. So, when it comes to trying to determine my life's purpose, I have to start with the Creator: The Dream Giver. Maybe you're thinking, "I don't know what God's dream is for my life." Or maybe you know, but are unsure of how to pursue it. Or perhaps you are forging full steam ahead towards the dream!

Wherever you are on the continuum, here are three things I've learned from my experience: **A. God's dream is always bigger than our own. B. God's dream goes beyond fame and fortune. C. God's dream will push us in the direction of our fear.**

A. God's dream is always bigger than our own... I didn't have any real dreams for my life as a teen. I had interests (like comics, drawing, airplanes and martial arts), but no clear focus. Even in college, I switched my major three times. There were also unexpected opportunities, which unearthed skills and talents I didn't know were in me!

One such example was digital filmmaking. I took my first television production class in college because my girlfriend (at the time) was taking it. Sure I loved watching television and films, but there was no burning desire within me to pursue entertainment production. I just wanted to be in the same room as my girlfriend! But when I took the class it was made abundantly clear that storytelling and the video production process was one of my talents.

After receiving "A's" in TV Production One and Two, I joked with my professor about being available if she ever needed me to teach her class. A few weeks later she asked me to teach her class while she was out of town at a media conference!

Since college, I have been able to combine my love for God with my love for media and produce a variety of documentaries, music videos, promotional infomercials, and independent films. Digital filmmaking has taken me across the country and around the world to seven African countries, China and Europe. Thank God for his amazing grace - to give a future to someone who felt like he had none!

B. God's dream goes beyond fame and fortune... I talk with many people whose driving force in life is making money and being famous. Having money is great - we need currency to get jobs done and to pay bills. And being known by others gives us a different kind of currency that helps us get things done as well. But, when our main dream in life revolves around money and fame and our self worth is determined by our possessions - it is easy to fall into a "false-identity" trap.

Jesus says in Luke 12:15, *"Take heed, and beware of covetousness: for a man's life consisteth not in the abundance of the things which he possesseth."* If this statement is true, then God's dream for our lives and how we determine our self-worth go way beyond fame and fortune!

Countless individuals have reached the top of the "fame and fortune" ladder and asked, "Is this all there is?" Many individuals in the public eye have fallen because they placed their identity in their status. Doesn't this show us that this type of living is unsustainable? God's ultimate dream for us will be something so deep in us that we are willing to pursue it even if we aren't lavished with money and notoriety. Why? Because God's dream for us brings something that wealth and status can't buy. God's purpose for us brings us fulfillment.

So does this mean we should be poor? Far from it. But it doesn't mean that we should spend our time on earth pursuing riches either. Proverbs 30:8-9 states, *"Remove falsehood and lies far from me; do not give me poverty or riches, feed me with my allotted portion of bread, lest I be full, and deny thee, and say, Who is the LORD? Or lest I be poor, and steal, and take the name of my God in vain."*

Author, Myles Monroe, shared in one of his books on pursuing purpose that, "whatever God has called us to do, he will provide the funds that correspond to the call." This directly relates to the Scripture from Proverbs. Seek God for his calling for your life and the resources that go with that calling. And then be diligent about being responsible with the resources that you have and watch what God does when you make your life and your resources available to him! Money can't buy you love, and it only does an okay job with securing you peace. But when you are pursuing the things God wants you to pursue, you will find yourself living in a state of fulfillment.

The last thing I wanted to do was be a preacher. My dad is a pastor, so I know from a son's perspective what it's like to be in ministry. But in college, God began calling me to preach, and I did everything I could to resist. However, through a series of non-coincidental events (which included a complete stranger, with no prior knowledge of me, speaking directly to my struggle) my path became clear. Do you know what happened to me? When God opened up opportunities for me to share the gospel, I would feel fulfilled. I had a sense of God's pleasure with my life. Preaching was not my dream, but it was a part of God's dream and purpose for my life.

C. God's dream will push us in the direction of our fear... My biggest battle in life has been with fear: fear of failure, fear of rejection, fear of success, fear of the unknown, fear of not being good enough, fear of pain and difficulty. Fear has kept me from making use of many opportunities. Fear has caused me to quit many endeavors. Fear has so terrorized my life, that I wrote a poem about it in my first book, *Transition: Breaking Through the Barriers.* (It's included in this book, at the beginning of the chapter on Fear.)

My undergraduate degree is in Speech Communication/Mass Communication. Although I knew this was the major for me (after trying two other majors) there still was one problem. I was an introvert (still am!), and very conscious about how others perceived me. I didn't particularly care for being in front of people. I didn't like being the center of attention. I would rather just stay in the background and go unnoticed. Yet, I felt compelled to major in Speech Communication (which had a high concentration of public speaking and debate classes). I can see, looking back, how God used my major to help me break out of my timid mold. After all, to be a preacher one must be able to speak publicly!

Public speaking was something that frightened me. On one such occasion, the entire communications department held an all-day forum to showcase student talent. I had unknowingly made college history as the first male student to become a Speech Communication major. When it was my turn to deliver my speech at the forum, my advisor made a huge introduction based on this historical fact. Her introduction and the fact that my speech followed my two female classmates left me terrified!

As I took the podium in front of a room full of professors and students, my hands and feet began to sweat. As my speech began, my heart was beating so hard it felt like it would burst through my chest! Nausea set as my vision started to distort and go black. My mouth felt like it was the Sahara desert, and my mind was screaming, "You are going to either throw up or pass out!" I started praying to God for help! And just at the point when embarrassment was imminent, a refreshing wave of energy washed over me! All of my symptoms immediately diminished, my confidence increased, and I was able to finish strong! God's dream for us may push us into an area that we fear. But it's okay to go there if he is leading us. He's not taking us there to fail, but to overcome, breakthrough and succeed. To reach our full potential, the area of our fear is often where we need to go.

AT SOME POINT...

Maybe at some point in your life you have felt unqualified, overwhelmed and unsure. Maybe you feel like that right now! That's okay! But you can't allow your feelings to keep you where you are. You CAN move to live out God's dream for your life!

God may not be calling us to go up against nations and political leaders. God may not be calling you to be a preacher. But whatever He desires for you to do will definitely be something beyond your imagination— something that will bring fulfillment to your life and take advantage of every gift, talent and skill that you have. And let me also say that the type of fulfillment I'm talking about isn't one free of opposition. Jesus said we'd have trouble in life, but we can take heart because he already overcame the world (John 16:33). The type of fulfillment that I am talking about comes despite opposition. So, even if you find yourself in chaotic situations, if you know that God has led you there, then you can rest in his pleasure for your life's purpose.

One of my favorite scripture verses is, *"Let your light so shine before men, that they may see your good works, and glorify your Father which is in heaven."* (Matthew 5:16)

Take some time to pray and think through this question: "What is God's dream for my life?" Write down whatever comes to mind to help you make sense of things. Maybe you have dreams for your life. Maybe you don't. Either way, you were created for a purpose, which begins and ends with knowing God and bringing Him glory. To begin our quest from any other point is to miss the key ingredient in building a life that is both successful and significant.

2. HOW CAN I PURSUE GOD'S DREAM FOR ME?

After you begin developing your relationship with God, the next thing you need to do is discover and develop your skills and talents. Discovering and then developing your skills and talents will provide indicators/landmarks to God's purpose for your life.

"A man's gift maketh room for him, and bringeth him before great men." (Proverbs 18:16)

"Seest thou a man diligent in his business? He shall stand before kings; he shall not stand before mean men." (Proverbs 22:29)

God has uniquely equipped each of us with talents. But we won't know what they are if we don't try new things. What do you think you'd be good at? Drawing? Photography? Public speaking? Science? Try those things. What do you think you'd be terrible at? *(You can make your own list.)* Try those things too. The results of both approaches may surprise you.

Another one of my favorite scriptures is, *"It is the glory of God to conceal a thing: but the honor of kings is to search out a matter."* (Proverbs 25:2)

We have been given the wonderful opportunity of going on a treasure hunt to find the "treasure" God has placed within each of us! Often times it's easy to see the potential in others while missing it in ourselves! There have been plenty of times when I have encouraged others to overcome their struggles and press towards their dreams; only to find myself struggling to believe that there's greatness in me that God wants to share with the world. This is one of the reasons why you should never go on treasure hunts alone. In life we need each other not just to survive, but also to thrive.

For example, when people see me draw, they are often amazed. But when I see my drawings, I think of half a dozen artists I know that make my work look like stick figures. For years, this mentality caused me to downplay my drawing skills, and, as a result of my insecurity, I haven't (yet) fully developed them. However, after talking to professional artists who I trust, who've been able to look at my work and provide constructive criticism, my new mentality is to use their art and suggestions as motivation to make my drawing skills as exceptional as possible. It took me having to be in community with others who were talented, skilled, and trustworthy for me to have a new perspective.

Life Point: As we seek to develop our talents, we must put ourselves in environments that are conducive to the desired result.

Another way to pursue your purpose is to learn how you learn. Learning is a fundamental characteristic of all achievement, progress, success, and significance. It is at the heart of human society and even animal life on earth. A person cannot navigate through the world without having to learn something. So, the more we learn, the more we are capable of doing and the more efficient we can become.

However, there are many obstacles that must be overcome if one is to engage in the process of learning. A key ingredient in this process is having an understanding of how we each learn.

It didn't take a rocket scientist for me to realize that numbers aren't my "thing." Math, once it got complicated, was always a struggle for me. I found myself failing pre-calculus in high school. I just couldn't get it! My mother had to intervene - since she knew my teachers - and set me up with extra help. Twice a week, I would meet my math teacher after school to go over lessons. At first I hated it, but after a while things were starting to make sense! With a lot of hard work I was able to bring my grade from "F" to "C". That was the best "C" I ever got!

So, math wasn't the easiest thing for me. (Although my younger brother absolutely thrives off of mathematical equations!) But art, music, English, and physical education were areas where I did very well! So, it was interesting, when I entered graduate school, to learn about the Multiple Intelligences Theory (MI), which helped to explain my experience.

My professor, Dr. Ellen Arnold, explained that MI was developed by cognition and education professor, Howard Gardener, and has been pursued by psychologists and educators worldwide. The theory (which some have built upon) basically states that human beings have eight different kinds of intelligence (Dr. Arnold calls them "Smarts") that reflect different ways of interacting with the world. Although we each have all eight intelligences, no two individuals have them in the same exact configuration. Each person has a unique combination—similar to our fingerprints. Here is the listing for the eight intelligences (or smarts) we ALL have. The following descriptions are excerpts from Dr. Arnold's book, *The MI Strategy Bank:*

Linguistic: Word Smart. This person likes to learn new vocabulary, play with words, read and write. A word-smart learner gets lost in reading; learns by hearing, reading, and writing; learns through language derivations; likes to read; likes to talk; listens well to others; masters languages easily; masters oral and written presentations; usually does well in traditional academic settings. (p. 30 - 31)

Mathematics: Numbers-Smart. This person likes to be precise, figure out relationships, have a special goal, and solve things. A number-smart learner applies math well; approaches tasks methodically; is analytical; is comfortable with numbers; is goal-oriented; is logical; is organized; is precise; likes comparisons; looks for the bottom line; manages money well; measures progress; sees things in sequence; simplifies things; thinks in concrete terms; thinks practically; works efficiently. (p. 39 - 41)

Musical: Music-Smart. This person likes to connect music to emotions; hears music in his or her head all the time; sings to him or herself; taps or moves to rhythms. A music-smart learner has strong auditory skills; learns best when information is in rhyme, rhythm, tune, or sound patterns; listens well; reacts to voice tone in others; relates concepts to rhymes, poems, and music; remembers music and lyrics easily; uses rhythmic speech; uses songs to understand concepts; *and their* vocal chords respond when listening to someone else singing. (p. 1 - 2)

Kinesthetic: Body-Smart. This person likes to build, experience, feel and touch, make things, and move. A body-smart learner does many things *(for example* acting, painting, sports); expresses competency *of ideas* through movement; is active; is athletic; is dramatic; is energetic, is involved physically; learns best when concretely doing what is being taught; likes variety; makes things; and thinks best when their body is moving. (p. 20 - 22)

Spatial/Visual: Picture-Smart. This person likes to do puzzles, draw, imagine, use color and visualize. A picture-smart learner creates images in their own mind; describes *things* in vivid detail; dreams in color a lot; enjoys using graphic organizers; has a strong sense of direction; is sensitive to color; learns through connecting images; needs to see information; prefers having a model; remembers pictures better than words; sketches, designs, fills in semantic organizers to create something; thumbs through pictures stored in the mind; turns shapes inside their head; and uses maps rather than sequential directions. (p.10 - 12)

Natural environment: Nature-Smart. This person likes to categorize, collect, grow, plant, relate to animals, and sort. A nature-smart learner cares about the environment; enjoys collecting natural objects *(like* rocks *and* leaves); has extensive knowledge about species or natural substances; is aware of changes in weather or growing patterns; learns best when relating new information to something in nature; likes to garden or farm; *and* shows sensitivity to animals. (p.67-69)

Intrapersonal: Self-Smart. This person likes to be alone; have time to think things through; reflect. A self-smart learner enjoys working alone; has few but close friends; is analytical; is independent; is a deep thinker; is meditative; is self-aware, likes to go last; needs time to reflect; prefers to work in quiet; thinks deeply. (p. 49 – 51)

Interpersonal: People-Smart. This person likes to be with people, empathize, interact, lead, teach. A people-smart learner actively participates in groups; communicates well; compromises well; is charismatic; is friendly; is giving; is outgoing; is perceptive; is persuasive; is sensitive to others' needs; leads others; likes to learn in groups; listens; nurtures; remembers characters from books or films; remembers stories about people; takes risks; talks a lot; thinks aloud; values relationships; wants feedback; works well with people. (p. 57-59)

DISCOVER YOUR ZONE!

What is your zone? How do you learn best? I discovered that the best way I learn is through my visual, music, linguistic, kinesthetic and intrapersonal smarts. I do use the other "smarts", but to a lesser degree. So, I tend to approach learning opportunities from that vantage point. Take some time to determine how you learn best and how you can incorporate those aspects into your learning process. Then, as you begin to implement them, watch your potential start to take off! Everything can be learned. You just have to know how best YOU learn in order to put you in the best position to excel in life.

3. HOW DO I OVERCOME OBSTACLES THAT STAND IN THE WAY OF MY DREAM?

Fear, low self esteem, depression. Family drama and trauma. Laziness and procrastination. Anger and ingratitude. Negative peer pressure and bullying. Financial distress. The list goes on for internal and external obstacles which can stand in the way of our dreams. The question is, "How do we approach the obstacles in front of us?"

Firstly, realize that the biggest obstacle to your advancement in life is not external, but internal. The most resistance you will ever encounter as you pursue your purpose won't come from your enemies and detractors. You are your biggest obstacle: your mentality affects how you view situations. Your viewpoint (perspective) affects how you self-talk. Your self-talk influences how you take action or refrain from taking action. And your actions impact the responses of those around you.

Life Point: We live and make decisions based on words.

We often defeat ourselves before ever encountering any real threat to our plans. And when we do encounter opposition, we falter when we start owning disproportionate criticisms. The world is full of people who disqualify themselves because they can't control their thought life.

Secondly, realize that when you approach an obstacle, there are often many ways to surmount it. You can climb over an obstacle, or go around it, or under it, or through it. You can even turn away from the obstacle and go in a different direction! It is very rare that you don't have any options when dealing with an obstacle. However, you must stop and take time to consider them. What you consider is what you better understand.

One of my favorite activities in gym class was the obstacle course. The obstacle course is a great demonstration about life and solutions-based thinking! While successfully completing the course is mainly about physical performance, it's also about mental performance - how you assess the approaching obstacle and what you say to yourself in the process to provide motivation and strategy. Sadly, my former middle school gym teacher told me that obstacle courses had been phased out of the curriculum due to student risk concerns. And when speaking to a group of teens, most of them had no idea what an obstacle course was!

The obstacle course helps you assess your abilities. It exposes your weak and strong points. It allows you to run against the only thing that ultimately matters: time. How best do you navigate with the time you are given? Obstacle courses can be fun. By extension, dealing with obstacles in your life doesn't have to drain your life.

How do we overcome our obstacles? By having a different perspective. We must train our minds to think differently... to have a solutions-seeking mentality rather than a victim mentality.

To have a new perspective may mean finding new environments that are conducive to developing a new mindset. Where do you go to get away and think? Some people run. Others take bubble baths. Others walk through the forest or go sit by a lake or an ocean. What do you do? And who do you hang around? Are your friends negative most of the time? If so, then it's time for new friends, because your life is greatly influenced by the people you consistently hang around.

As you begin to change your perspective, you will also need to change the way you communicate. Make a list of people you trust - parent, teacher, pastor, mentor, etc. - and reach out to them for assistance. When I say trust, I mean talking to a person who not only won't put your business out in the street, but who also has your best interests at heart. This trustworthy person will desire your advancement in life and won't be afraid to encourage you while providing constructive criticism when necessary.

To overcome obstacles you must also take different actions. Actually, you've already begun taking a different action by reading this book! That's a great start! My pastor, Dr. Shellie Sampson, Jr., often says, *"You cannot solve a problem while remaining on the same level as the problem."* The actions that brought you to the obstacle cannot be the same actions that will take you beyond the obstacle. So, it's time to think differently!

There will always be obstacles. But obstacles can be turned into stepping-stones.

4. HOW CAN I HELP OTHERS REALIZE THEIR GOD-GIVEN DREAMS?
True success isn't about only amassing wealth and possessions for ourselves. Success is also about helping others reach their goals and become better individuals. We become who we are supposed to be while helping others on their life journey.

Ask about their dreams. Help them identify and develop their talents. Speak encouraging words. Help research their dreams. Share opportunities. These simple actions can have an impact on someone else that can literally change the course of their life. Speaking encouraging words is HUGE because we each deal with our own negative self talk every day.

There's an African proverb, which states, "If you want to go fast, go alone. But if you want to go far, go together." You will always be able to do more when you have the right people around you. Treat others like you would like to be treated and be the "right" person to help others in their pursuit of significance.

Here are five-steps to consider as you pursue success and significance. I call this a Five-Step Pursuit Plan!

1. To pursue God's dream for your life, begin studying what interests you - including ways to master your skills and talents. What interests you may not interest me, and that's OK because we are unique. Becoming adept at your interests helps to make you a confident, well-rounded individual who is able to interact in various social settings. Don't be afraid if you are interested in something most people are not. Discover what you are passionate about and begin to pursue it! Even if you end up not following your interests in the future, the process of learning them will yield many lessons, which could prove useful to you.

2. To pursue God's dream for your life, you must discover your "dream requirements." What do you want to do with your life? Be a marine biologist? A doctor? A songwriter? An executive chef? An astronaut? It's cool to talk about our dreams! It sounds good when we verbalize what we want to become! But it's also easy to hide behind our dream and remain at only the "talking phase." It's time to move from talking to action! Whatever career path you want to pursue, it's time to do your research on the process it takes to become what you desire.

While speaking at a teen forum I asked about career goals. Many teens had great aspirations, but when I asked about the steps required for them to reach their career goals, most of them had no clue.

What type of additional education will pursuing your dream require? Do you need to go to college or graduate school? Will you need to take an internship? Can you do an intensive certification workshop series over the course of a weekend or few weeks? Can you learn everything you need to know from watching instructional videos on the Internet? How much will pursuing your dream cost?

Maybe after you research your dream, you'll say, "No, that's not for me." Or maybe you'll say, "Alright! Let's move forward!" But you won't know until you take the step and research. Find out what your dream requires and you will be in a better position to make an informed decision about your life and destiny.

3. If you want to pursue God's dream for your life, you can also learn from someone living your dream. You can choose to learn on your own or through someone else. Sometimes, the most efficient way is to learn by observing others. Find a mentor. Take a tour. Volunteer. At least schedule a meeting with someone who is doing what you would like to do. Ask them questions about what it's like to do what they do: struggles, victories, and pitfalls to avoid.

I remember listening to a seminar done by Jim Rohn - America's foremost business philosopher - and he suggested that if a person wanted to do better in life, they should find a very wealthy individual and offer to take them to dinner. Most people will think that the rich person should buy their own dinner. But if you are willing to save up and pay to take a wealthy person to dinner and inquire about their philosophy for life and wealth; that person will most likely say something during the course of dinner that will completely change your life.

Learning from someone who's been where you want to go helps you to avoid costly mistakes on your journey. There's no need for you to reinvent the wheel if it's already been invented. (Although, there are times when your interactions may lead to an idea for *improving* the wheel!) So, learn from those who have already gone ahead of you. One thing I like to do when I can't meet someone who is living the dream I aspire to, is read about him or her and study his or her work. As a filmmaker, one of my favorite study techniques is to watch the behind-the-scenes features on movies that inspire me. This way I can learn about filmmakers whom I have yet to meet.

4. To pursue God's dream for your life you definitely need to be a good manager of your money! I have been a very poor manager of money down through the years. I can laugh now because after much heartache and newfound purpose, I am on the disciplined path to financial success! It is said that, "hindsight is 20/20." I can't go back and do things differently, but I can learn from the past and make better decisions today in order to have a better future!

Seriously... Having control over how you spend, invest and save is critical to the success of your God-given dream. There will be times when you will have to invest in your dream, but if your finances are in disarray, you won't be able to - at least not without going into debt. A constant reminder of failure for me - down through the years - has been my finances. Sadly, many of us don't grow up with a thorough knowledge about the value of money and how to make it work in our favor. I was one such person. It was easy to spend money - easier than saving and investing. College credit cards introduced me to a downward financial spiral of overwhelming debt. When family came to bail me out, it wasn't very long before I was back in debt again. Why? Because my mentality about debt and money had not changed.

Now let me say that I did pay my bills. But the use of my discretionary income was questionable at times. I enjoyed buying things. And if I didn't have the cash, I would just charge it. Since I was employed, there was money coming in, but in reality we were living paycheck to paycheck. On payday, the money would often be gone as soon as it came in. And according to statistics, nearly one-third of Americans are just one paycheck away from poverty.

After being unemployed for just over a year in 2012, while trying to take care of my wife and son, I hit a financial low that I had never experienced before! Once I began working again I knew that a life of financial distress was unacceptable. I hadn't done enough to prepare for tough times. It was time to become more financially responsible. After much prayer and reading financial help materials like Dave Ramsey's *Financial Peace*, I am making informed financial decisions to put my family in a better position to capitalize on future opportunities.

Another aspect of maintaining financial responsibility is to have a dream to focus on. When you have goals you want to accomplish and have attached a dollar amount to each goal, it's easier to resist impulse buying, while increasing your saving and investing options. I imagine the day when my family is completely debt free - owing no credit cards and no student loans! I look forward to being able to take the thousands we pay our creditors and be able to invest fully in our dreams to change the world. If you want to pursue your God-given dreams, you must become financially responsible.

5. To pursue God's dream for your life you need to take care of your body, mind and spirit. What's the use of pursuing your purpose if you won't take care of yourself? What's the point of getting your dream job, if your body is falling apart due to poor eating habits and a lack of exercise? Why should someone give you a fantastic opportunity if your mindset is pessimistic and limiting? Who should put their trust in you if you're not even at peace with yourself?

It is often said that, "Success happens when preparation meets opportunity." So, we must make sure that we prepare for our dreams in a holistic manner that will help ensure that we can take advantage of opportunities when they present themselves. Jim Rhon stated in a motivational seminar that, *"Many people don't do well because they don't feel well!"* How would your life look if you could exercise your body, mind and spirit on a regular basis every week? How much more vitality would you have? What type of strategy can you put in place to make sure that your personal development is a priority? You are no good to anyone else if you don't take a holistic approach to your own personal development.

Life Point: Your body serves as the vehicle through which you live out your purpose. Maximize yourself and you increase your chances of fulfilling your destiny.

MOVING TIPS!

- We navigate the world through questions.

- Asking the right questions is one key to success.

- God's dream is always bigger than our own. God's dream goes beyond fame and fortune. God's dream will often push us in the area of our fear.

- We live out our purpose through our bodies.

- We live and make decisions based on words.

- We become who we are supposed to be while helping others on their life journey.

- Find out what your dream requires and you will be in a better position to make an informed decision about your life and destiny.

- Your body serves as the vehicle through which you live out your purpose. Maximize yourself and you increase your chances of fulfilling your destiny.

- Your success and significance in life is tied to the genuine relationships you have with others. While pursuing your dreams, you become better as you help others to do the same.

- As we seek to develop our talents, we must put ourselves in environments that are conducive to the desired result.

GET MOVING!

Here are questions and key thoughts that can help you move forward.

A. Which environments propel your learning process?

B. Which type of learner are you?

C. How are YOU your biggest obstacle? How can you overcome your issues?

D. List everyone who loves, supports and tells you the truth.

E. How are you working to bring all areas of your life into proper balance?

CHAPTER 4:
Hiding In Plain Sight!

ONE TIME I WAS RUNNING LATE FOR A FLIGHT... As my parents dropped me off at the airport, my mother told me to call her after I had made it through the security checkpoint. I got to the gate with a few minutes to spare and called my mom on my cell phone. While talking to her, I began to make sure I had everything. Suddenly, I was frantic.

"Aw, Man!" I said as I checked my pockets and suitcase.

"What's the matter?" my mother asked.

I replied with great trepidation, "I can't find my phone! I think I left it at the security checkpoint!"

My mother was quiet for a second before responding, "Aren't you talking to me on your phone?"

We both laughed!

Have you ever been looking for something that was hiding in plain sight? Oftentimes, truth is this way. We say we don't know what to do, but after talking with someone else we realize that we knew the truth all along... but we were just afraid to act on it. But there are times when we don't know the truth about a situation; where we genuinely don't know what our next step should be. This is when we need to take advantage of a great life opportunity. We must open our mouths and ask for help.

The A.S.K. Principle (Matthew 7:7-8)

To be both successful and significant, we must approach life with an A.S.K. attitude. I call this the A.S.K. Principle. In Matthew 7, verses 7-8: Jesus states, *"Ask, and it shall be given you; seek, and ye shall find; knock, and it shall be opened unto you; For every one that asketh receiveth; and he that seeketh findeth; and to him that knocketh it shall be opened."*

The power of asking is huge! Taking advantage of asking will make a difference in the number of opportunities we are able to capitalize on. Here's an example: I have been in two situations where what I wanted at a store was not out on the shelf. My first thought was, "I guess they're out of stock." My second thought was, "I should ask just in case they have some in the back." In both situations, there were more items in the back that just didn't make it to the sales floor. So, I walked away with what I wanted. But how many people before or after me, wanted the same thing, saw the empty space on the shelf and didn't ask if there were any more left? How many people walked away with their desire unfulfilled?

The very word **"ASK"** serves as an acronym for the process: Ask. Seek. Knock. I was amazed when this realization hit me during the early months of 2013! I had read this passage countless times over the years and never saw the truth that was hiding in plain sight! Jesus lets us know that this is how we should approach life. And in these two verses he presents a "drill-down" effect.

ASK: everyone asks questions at some point in their lives. The inference here also is that if we don't ask, nothing will be given. No opportunity comes without some kind of request. So, asking is top-level, something we all do. And when we ask genuine questions we end up receiving genuine answers as we continue the process.

SEEK: Fewer people are in this category. Asking a question is a great beginning, but there comes a point when we each must decide if we will pursue what we are asking about. Will we pursue what we need as if we were looking for buried treasure? "Seeking" means leaving where we are to go to where our answer might be. Are we willing to take the risk and leave our comfort zone, fears, and any other issue we may have in order to seek "what could be?"

KNOCK: Even fewer people knock on the door of opportunity when they get to it! So, we've asked; and then we've gotten up off our butts and went seeking for our solution. Now our journey has led us to a door where what we need and desire is right on the other side. We're like Neo from the first Matrix film, when Morpheus brings him to the apartment of the oracle and tells him, "I can only bring you to the door. You are the one who has to walk through it."

Jesus tells a parable in Luke 18: 1-8 about the persistent widow who goes to a judge to seek justice against her adversary. When she comes the first time, the judge does nothing. He could care less about her situation. But she doesn't let up. She "knocks" on the judge's door daily and repeatedly asks him to take action on her behalf. Eventually, because of her continual "asking, seeking, and knocking" he heeds her request! Her request was valid. But sometimes, a valid request isn't enough to get people to move. Sometimes, for things to happen it takes persistence!

But how many of us are like the widow? In fact, many of us are just the opposite. And this is where we freeze... at the door where the answer to our question is waiting; where the provision for our need is waiting; where even more questions are waiting. We are right at the door... and we freeze. I've been there - several times. Here's a story about one such time.

Flyer Failure

On my bookshelf is a stack of flyers that were never mailed out. As an author, I had the opportunity to promote my first novel, *Speedsuit Powers*, to a wide list of people and venues. I had already "asked" for help with putting a mailing list together. I already did my "seeking" and found a graphic artist who designed an excellent, professional looking flyer. And as I stood, ready to knock at the door of opportunity - I froze. My negative self-talk kicked in: "What if I send this mailing out and get no response?" "What if I send this mailing out and get too many responses and can't meet the demand?" "What if people and groups ask me to speak and I have nothing valuable to say?" "What if I suddenly get stage fright while speaking to a group or on television or radio?"

The negative self-talk of "What if" is one of the quickest ways to smother your dreams before they even have a chance to surface! This is why we need to take control over our thought life! Until talking to a friend about the situation, I only thought my inaction was just that - inaction. As it turned out, my decision not to knock and walk through the door of opportunity was costly. It cost me opportunities, potential income, and the possibility of impacting hundreds, if not thousands of lives! Fear had robbed me... but I was an accessory to the crime. So, the flyers on my bookshelf now serve as an object lesson. They remind me of my failure; but also of my possibility.

By the way - that story about being in the stores with empty shelves - in both situations when I initially asked if there were more in the back, the employee told me "No." After asking if they could check to be sure, they came back with the product I wanted. It wasn't that they were trying to hide the merchandise; they just didn't know it was there.

Having an A.S.K. attitude is ultimately about follow-through. Many of us are great "starters" but terrible "finishers." Many of us have one area of our lives together, while other areas are in shambles. The world is full of people who live and die without ever fully maximizing their potential. We come up with ideas, plans and strategies that we never implement or haphazardly carry out. Do you want to be part of that group? Or would you rather be part of the group that, while on the way to maximizing their potential, gives others the permission to do the same?

MOVING TIPS!

- The negative self-talk of "What if" is one of the quickest ways to smother your dreams before they even have a chance to surface! This is why we must control our thought life!

- We must approach life with an A.S.K. attitude: Ask - Seek - Knock.

- Then we must follow through with our actions, as well as learn from our in-action.

GET MOVING!

Here are questions and key thoughts that can help you move forward.

A. How can you approach life from an Ask – Seek – Knock perspective?

B. In your life, when have you been persistent?
   When have you given up?

C. How does negative self-talk neutralize your attempts to move forward?

D. In what ways are you an accessory to the crime of your lost dreams?

E. In what ways does your lost dream affect more people than just you?

F. How can you use what you are learning to propel you forward?

CHAPTER 5:
Overcoming Obstacles

UNKNOWN FEAR

I know you're out there. I've felt you most of my life…
Lurking around the corners and in the shadows
Slithering your way into my mind.
For so long you've kept me running
Running away from where I was supposed to be
Running away from things I was supposed to see
You kept me so afraid that I missed so many opportunities.
You were always unknown… but somehow I knew who you were.
"What if I can't do it?" You'd whisper in my ear. "What if I fail?"
I used to buy into your manipulating suggestions
And your downright bullying
Anytime I tried to press through.
I remember how I used to feel… so afraid
Like I couldn't do anything but fail.
I felt so inadequate… so small… Unprepared.
Vulnerable… naked.
Yes. I remember how you used to make me feel
Like I was supposed to live my whole life in you… Fear.
You lied to me! But that's what you do.
Never would I have guessed in a thousand lifetimes
That it is really you who are afraid.
Terrified of me – That I would fulfill the exact purpose
For which I was created.

Transition: Breaking Through the Barriers, Pg. 101.
Written by: Allen Paul Weaver III
Published by: IUniverse June 2006

OBSTACLE COURSE

I LOVE OBSTACLE COURSES! (I said that before.) We did a lot of them in middle school: crawling through tubes, quickly stepping through tires, swinging from rope to rope, climbing over walls... Obstacle courses were my favorite activity in gym class! (My second favorite was track and field.) I was a skinny string-bean-of-a-kid back then: not really built for football, not fluid enough for basketball, nor acrobatic enough for gymnastics. But when it was time for the obstacle course... I flew through it relatively uninhibited! Sure, my friends, and enemies, and I were trying to get the best time with the fewest mistakes. But one of the reasons I loved the challenge was because completing the obstacle course meant that my only two real opponents were the clock and myself.

Ultimately, life is much the same way. We may spend time trying to tackle someone else or block his or her shots. Someone may spend time trying to do the same to us; but our biggest competitors are not others. Our biggest competitors are ourselves, and time. When we think about overcoming obstacles, we have to realize that we can be our greatest ally or our greatest enemy. How we deal with the baggage of our own fears, doubts and insecurities will greatly determine what we accomplish in life. How we manage the time we've been given will determine the quality level of what we accomplish before we die.

Realize that the obstacles you face in life need to be viewed as a type of "course." They are present not so much to cause you to fail (although some people may present them for that reason). You see; obstacles are tests... And what do tests do? Tests show you where you are. Tests reveal your strengths and weaknesses. Tests show where you could be if you applied yourself. They also show where you'll be if you refuse to grow. A good teacher gives tests to the student in the hopes that they will succeed.

Several years ago I came to the realization that people are born with baggage. We have baggage inherited from our parents. We have baggage inherited from the environment that we grow up in. Our task is to learn how to transform our "baggage" situations from issues that slow us down to fuel that propels us forward! Also, there is a difference between baggage and luggage. On a journey, too much baggage can slow us down greatly. But, having the right amount of luggage to carry our necessities helps us move forward on the journey more efficiently.

The obstacles you face in life have the potential to break you. But they can also help you grow and develop your mind, body and spirit. The difference between success and failure rests primarily on your ability to see things from a positive perspective. See your obstacles for what they really are and then confront them one by one. Running away from obstacles turns them into baggage that will drag you down. Confronting them will help you transform your obstacles into something that will benefit you and those around you.

Sadly, in 2011 while visiting my old middle school, the gym teacher said they no longer did obstacle courses, due to liability issues. What a shame! Obstacle courses taught me so much. How much are our kids missing without them?

WHAT'S HOLDING YOU BACK?

Think about this question for a moment. What obstacle is holding you back from moving from where you are to where you need and want to be? Maybe it's the following. Check all that apply.

Fear/Insecurity:
Lack of knowledge/know-how/plan/strategy:
Distractions/Illusions:
Lack of resources:
Time management:
Other people:
Negative self-talk:
Anger management: (or other types of emotional instability)
Procrastination:
Perfectionism:
Comfort zone:
Your body:

Here is a PROCESS to help you address your obstacles: 1) Determine the places you get stuck. 2) Understand why you get stuck. 3) Develop ways to get unstuck. Let's look at each issue. I want you to list your specific circumstance for each. Then answer the questions and determine how you can take positive action.

ASSESSMENT QUESTIONS

1. What type of fear/insecurity are you facing? (failure, uncertainty, etc...)

2. What information don't you know that you feel you need to know?

3. What 'time stealers' distract you from reaching your goals?

4. What resources do you think you need?

5. How do you allow others to keep you from moving forward in life?

6. How does your internal "speak" hold you back?
   What do you say to yourself?

7. What types of situations really push your buttons?
   Why do they bother you?

8. What type of situations cause you to procrastinate?

9. How does perfectionism affect you?

10. In what ways does wanting to be comfortable keep you stagnant?

11. How does an illness, injury or disability keep you from pursuing your goals?

12. What areas do you feel you've already mastered?

13. What are other reasons for not moving which are not listed here?

SOLUTION-BASED-QUESTIONS

1. What steps can you take to overcome fear/insecurity?

2. How can you learn what you need to know?

3. How can you increase your focus so you are not distracted from your goals?

4. How can you better manage your time and resources so they work for you?

5. How can you pursue your dream with a 5-30 minute block of time each day?

6. What methods can you use to counteract the negative impact of others on you?

7. How can you transform your self-talk from negative to positive?

8. How can you reward non-procrastination behavior to decrease bad habits?

9. How can you make sure perfectionism doesn't slow your momentum?

10. How can you increase your comfort zone tolerance?

11. How can you 'MOVE!' while dealing with a restrictive physical condition?

12. How can you be a perpetual learner?

A FEW WORDS

Did you know more about the solutions to your issues than you realized? That is the beauty of asking the right questions; they often illuminate our journey. I wanted you to tackle these first before I shared a few quick thoughts.

A. Ultimately, no matter what your issues are, the one thing that's holding you back in life - more than any other factor - is you. This was stated earlier. History is full of people who overcame seemingly insurmountable external odds because they were internally committed, focused, and consistent about pursuing a higher ideal than what they were currently experiencing. We have to take responsibility for our actions and inactions. Many times we are our own worst enemy. Having said that - when we apply truth and discipline to our lives we can become our own ally. Just look at the previous questions. I am making an assumption, but if you took the time to answer them, you most likely figured out some practical solutions to your issues. However, your problem isn't necessarily a lack of information - but rather a lack of implementation. The benefit only comes when we take the truth that we know and apply it.

B. There is a way to overcome every negative experience we face: by having positive experiences that connect to our area of struggle. Author and life coach, Valorie Burton, states in her book, Successful Women Think Differently, "Negative emotion is more psychologically powerful than positive. When you have a negative experience, it takes more than just one equally positive experience to bounce back. Negative emotion causes powerful physiological changes in the body and mind. Reversing those changes requires more than an equal dose of positive emotion. In fact, it takes about three positive experiences to balance the effects of one negative experience."

C. No one wants to be around someone who can't manage his or her emotions and mental state. Being around such a person is mentally and physically draining. And when our emotions are out of control, we do and say things that will cost us opportunities and bring regret. Just take a look at Moses. He had an anger management issue. His lack of control caused him to not be allowed entrance into the land God had prepared for his people. You see, Moses had a good reason to be angry: the people were rebelling against God. But Moses allowed his anger to cause him to sin when he disobeyed a direct command of God in front of the entire congregation. And he had to live with the consequences. (Numbers 20:1-12)

D. A change in perspective will change your life. No matter what you are going through, there are always others who are facing worse situations. And there are those who have learned how to transform their area of deficiency into an area of dominance. Here are two examples of such individuals who don't let their physical handicap keep them from living life and pursuing their purpose: Dr. Steven

Hawking and Nick Vujicic. While Steven Hawking is known for his lack of faith in God, he is also known for two other things: being the most brilliant theoretical physicist since Einstein and (even more impressive) not allowing his motor neuron disease (which has restricted him to a wheel chair and taken away his speech) keep him from pursuing his passions. And then there's Nick Vujicic. He is an Australian evangelist, motivational speaker, author, husband and father who travels the world inspiring others towards their God-given greatness. But that's not the absolutely amazing part. Nick was born with Tetra-Amelia syndrome, a rare disorder that caused him to be born without all four of his limbs. His mantra in life is: "From No Limbs To No Limits!"

E. The human brain is designed to adapt to different circumstances and stimuli. God has given us the ability to break through and break free - if we are willing to trust Him with our life and put in the effort that's required to change. With proper effort, discipline, and instruction, we can unlearn many habits that diminish our lives, and replace them with habits that will develop our existence into something spectacular. One part of this transformation happens when we take time to self-reflect in order to understand the motivations behind the things we do. Another part happens when we actively replace our negative thinking with truthful statements. Fears and bad habits don't have to hold you back. Emotional instability and physical disability don't have to keep you from moving forward and diving deeper into life. It's time to Move! Your destiny is waiting on you!

OVERCOMING FEAR

I stated earlier in this book that my biggest battle in life has been with fear. There have been two recent major situations in my life where fear has been a huge issue.

The first situation was when I produced my first independent feature film (Speedsuit) during the summer of 2011. There were so many obstacles—loss of a major investor, loss of my director of photography, difficulties getting key locations, and my editing computer crashing! I wanted to quit, but there were people around me who believed in me and in the project's potential. So we pressed through every obstacle and amazingly found provision on the other side of every challenge.

My second major life challenge was when I was unemployed for 13 months. Due to a round of layoffs, I lost my job at the end of January 2012. For the next 13 months, I could not find work. I encountered fear on an entirely new level as I had to be concerned not just about my welfare, but the welfare of my wife and our 2 year-old son. I had never been so low financially, as I was about six months into being unemployed. We had no savings and the bills kept mounting higher and higher. If not for the grace of God and the help of family and friends, fear would have overtaken me and we would have been out on the streets! I am happy to say that at the end of the 13 months a job opportunity opened up for me and it has been one of the best working experiences that I have had in a very long time!

Even while in the midst of these two recent situations, I learned a lot more about God, life, faith, discipline and perseverance. As the saying goes, "What does not kill you only serves to make you stronger." I would add, "stronger if you open yourself to learn the lesson." Don't let tough situations make you bitter. Let tough situations make you better! In the process of my struggles, when I wanted to give up on everything, there were five things I would do to help me move forward.

I know I am not alone in my struggle with fear, so let me share these five steps in an effort to help you overcome your fears. What you are about to read is the transcript from a video blog post I did in February in response to a challenge given by Brendon Burchard - hailed as "One of the top business and marketing trainers in the world." His challenge was to do a "5 Step" how-to video on anything as a way of demonstrating that all of us have the ability to say things that matter. I was afraid to accept the challenge. That's when I had an epiphany, "I'll do a video about overcoming fear!" So, here's what I said – with some additional comments:

5 STEPS TO OVERCOME FEAR...

Often it is fear - more than any other emotion - that derails our destiny. Now, I'm not talking about that healthy sense of fear that says "don't stick your wet finger into an electrical socket" or "don't go stand in front of an oncoming car." I am talking about that OTHER type of fear. YOU know what it is. The kind where we look back on our lives and see many things we could have done - but didn't do - not because we didn't have the opportunity... but because we were afraid. But fear does not have to rule our lives any longer! The more we face our fears - the less fearful they become. And here are FIVE things you can do to overcome fear and have a better life as a result.

1. Understand that fear is a choice.

In his film, After Earth, Will Smith has a quote, "Danger is real. Fear is a choice." Many of us are afraid of situations that are not dangerous, but merely uncomfortable, new, and unknown to us - but not necessarily to others. Danger does not automatically mean failure, but being fearful will most certainly lead to diminished capacity. When we choose to be fearful, we close ourselves off from seeing solutions to our problems. We place ourselves in a chokehold. If you want to be significant, you must understand that fear is a choice.

2. Own your fear.

By this I mean, do not let your fear dictate your actions. In order to do this you have to OWN it! You have to look your fear in the face and begin to understand the motivation behind your fear. When you understand the motivation behind your fear, you can determine if it is valid or not. But how do you know what the motivating factors are? You ask yourself, "Why am I afraid of this situation? Then be open and honest with about the answer! Then you can create a course of action for making sure that the fear does not paralyze you. You own your fear and not the other way around.

3. Learn to "Press through Fear."
Most people we deem as courageous (the firefighter, police officer, surgeon, soldier, public speaker) will tell you that they are often afraid while doing certain aspects of their jobs. It's normal to be afraid when the outcome is unknown. After all we're human. But it is abnormal to allow ourselves to remain in fear. Courage is not the absence of fear, but doing what needs to be done even while you're afraid. As we "press through the fear" it will diminish.

4. Hang around others who have overcome their fears.
I had a more than healthy fear of water when I was in middle school. It was one of my mother's gifts to me. My dad was a strong swimmer and one day we were at a backyard cookout, standing by the poolside, talking with the lifeguard. My dad said, "My son doesn't know how to swim. He's too afraid to learn." The lifeguard looked at me and said, "You don't know how to swim?" The next thing I saw was blue sky and puffy white clouds just before being swallowed up whole by the backyard pool! I fought to get to the surface and thrashed around in the water! I cried out for help and the lifeguard said, "Stand up!" He had thrown me in the four-foot section. I was over five feet tall. I yelled, "What'd you do that for?" He and my dad started laughing as he said, "How else were you going to overcome your fear of water?" In reality, I wasn't in any real danger. All I had to do was stand up. And if I couldn't there were two strong swimmers ready to jump in the water to rescue me.

If you hang around those who have overcome their fears, you will most likely do the same. Just don't be surprised when they throw you into the pool.

5. Pray.
The Bible states, "For God hath not given us the spirit of fear; but of power, and of love, and of a sound mind." 2 Timothy 1:7. We may become afraid, but we are not to stay afraid. Pray and ask God to give you the strength to overcome your fears and to use the tools that are at your disposal to do so. Often, our fears are tied into our perceived inability; but God's Word states that we have been given power (capability

- the ability to be successful in the areas that we apply ourselves in), love (we are not alone - nor abandoned - in our struggles), and a sound mind (the ability to reason out a situation for what it really is - thereby nullifying fear at its root.)

I have just shared with you 5 ways to overcome fear. If you put these steps into action, you will begin to see positive change in your life. Remember, it's not about being fearless... it's about fearing less.

MOVING TIPS!

- How you deal with YOU will greatly determine your accomplishments in life. How you manage your time will determine the quality of your accomplishments.

- Understand that fear is a choice. And you have the tools to overcome it.

- Our biggest competitors are not others. Our biggest competitors are ourselves, and the time we have on earth.

- Tests show you where you are. They reveal your strengths and weaknesses and show where you could be if you applied yourself. They also show where you'll be if you refuse to grow.

- The benefit only comes when we take the truth that we know and apply it.

- Running from obstacles turns them into baggage, which will drag you down. Confronting obstacles transforms them into luggage that benefits you and those around you.

- Become a perpetual learner! What we feel we've already mastered, we don't work on.

- DETERMINE the places you get stuck. UNDERSTAND why you get stuck. DEVELOP ways to get unstuck.

GET MOVING!

Here are questions and key thoughts that can help you move forward.

A. How do you deal with your fears and doubts?

B. How can you replace the strategies that don't work?

C. What obstacles are keeping you from moving?

D. How can you incorporate '5 Steps to Overcome Fear' into your own life?

CHAPTER 6:
Moving Forward

SUCCESS IS ABOUT ACHIEVING GOALS. Significance is about pursuing goals that positively impact the lives of others. To lead a fulfilling life, a person needs both success and significance. The last thing I want (for you or me) is that you get to the end of your life and discover that you were busy living out the expectations of people rather than the dreams that God had for you. I don't want your life to be filled with regrets about what could have been if you had only had the courage and discipline to take action.

Which will you do? Will you stand on the sidelines of life and watch positive growth opportunities pass you by? Or will you actively participate in the development of your own life? I have a list of regrets - some I have shared in this book. But, by God's grace, I have turned that list into a means of motivation for living out my future as I journey to become all that God has intended and desired for me to be. I also have a growing list of new experiences! Here is one such experience below. Let me first say that this book was already written before the experience happened, but once it happened I knew the story of how it came about needed to be included in this book!

CHASING UNEXPECTED DREAMS:
A Comedic Journey Case Study

Some dreams we choose: we see a person doing something that's amazing or intriguing to us and we think to ourselves, "I would like to try that!" We go after these dreams. We plan for them - set goals and action steps. We put ourselves in environments where we can make contact with those who are already living the dream. We ask questions and try the dream out.

Then there are unexpected dreams... These dreams sneak up on us—or rather 'in' us. We see people living out a particular dream a thousand times and never have a desire to try it. In some cases we may even fear trying it. And then one day... everything changes.

This is what happened to me. About a year or two ago, a small, quiet desire began to swell up inside of me. Somehow, I wanted to try Stand-Up Comedy. This was a very much-unexpected dream because I grew up NOT being funny. Ask any of my childhood friends and they ALL will insist that I was corny. At best I had one good funny story maybe once every two to four months. At worst - many of my friends often laughed 'at' me and not 'with' me.

But somehow, as I got older, I became funnier! But still, never enough to consider doing Stand-Up. And even today, my wife thinks I am pretty corny!

So imagine my surprise as this unexpected dream accosted me! So, for the last year and a half, I sat on the growing dream and barely mentioned it to anyone. My intention was to smother it to death, but it has turned out to be more like a hen that sits on its eggs—waiting for them to hatch. Only, I didn't know I was waiting...

An Unexpected Opportunity...

Then an unexpected opportunity presented itself. My job was having an All-Staff Conference. An email revealed that among the lineup of events, would be a talent show and volunteer participants were needed. At first, I couldn't think of any known talents to display in front of a gathering of 100-200 people. Then I remembered this unexpected dream.

It took a week for me to consider whether or not to follow this dream. I was in the middle of a tug-of-war! On one side was the fear. On the other side was the dream. And there was me—right in the middle! Somehow, I forced myself to reply to the email—stating that I would participate. Then a long internal battle ensued as I wrestled with self-doubt and the reality of my past track record of corniness. "What had I done?" "Was I out of my mind?" I was panicking and thought about recanting my participation, but when I was about to do so, the 'egg' of this unexpected dream cracked!

At the point when my terror was at its highest, a thought entered my mind: "what better place to try comedy for the very first time than in an environment filled with people you know?"

So, I began working with my wife to pull a routine together. As the weeks passed, we honed and tweaked it (and my wife spent a lot of time making fun of me). Then coworkers began to find out about my upcoming comedy routine, and excitement among staff began to build. As it did for them, terror—once again—began to build for me. But there was no going back. Expectations were high and I would either fail miserably or succeed exceptionally in front of a large room full of people!

It's Time to MOVE!
This journey became an exercise of faith for me as I literally walked out the steps and thought pattern of this book! As my terror mounted, I said to myself, "I can't release a book on overcoming fear, maximizing challenges and turning obstacles into opportunities - and then not take advantage of this opportunity to perform Stand-Up Comedy."

The day finally arrived and the nervousness remained until the moment before the performance. I prayed (as I had been throughout this whole journey) for God's blessing and guidance. "Lord, I believe You placed this desire in me. Let me have fun with this and may You be glorified."

Living the Dream...
My name was called, "And now, here is Laughing With Allen!" It was now or never! As soon as my feet landed on the stage, my nervousness vanished and I walked into the reality of an unexpected dream... The dream lasted 16 minutes; and there were some mistakes - but it felt as if the moment was created just for me.

When it was over and everyone was clapping and cheering, I thought about what it would have been like if I had allowed my fear to keep me from chasing this unexpected dream... An opportunity to see the world and myself in a new light would have been lost—perhaps forever. But now I know what is on the other side of fear and nervousness: the potential for both failure and success… and the gracious gift of learning from the journey and inspiring others in the process.

I don't know where Stand-Up Comedy will take me (if anywhere). But I do know that whatever happens—if doors open or close—I will enjoy the journey.

Your Choice…
Life is too short to allow fear to keep you from pursuing the deep dreams that live within you. Whether they be dreams you chose first or dreams that seemed to choose you; just be ready to say "yes" when an opportunity presents itself. Even if you have no idea how the dreams will come about, don't stop believing. Don't stop making preparations. Don't stop praying. Proverbs 3 tells us, if we trust God and don't lean on our own understanding - but rather acknowledge him in all of our ways - then he will direct our paths.

Dreams don't happen just because we want them to. They happen when we work towards them and take advantage of opportunities that encourage their expression.

Let me share a 2008 blog post with you as I conclude this book. This is from my APW3. com site. Little did I know then, that this post would be the seed, which would eventually grow into the book you are now reading.

"DESTINY IS WAITING ON US" (formerly posted on February 6, 2008)

"Destiny is waiting on us…" My Writing Accountability Partner, Dr. Tisha Y. Lewis, spoke these words to me after hearing about my speaking opportunity at Bethune-Cookman University in January 2007: I was able to dialogue with Communication and Theater Arts students about linking their experience with opportunities while sharing from my book, *Transition: Breaking Through the Barriers.* This was an exciting and uncomfortable time. It was exciting because speaking here was one of my dreams! It was uncomfortable because I had never done it before!

Yet through the mixed emotions, there was fulfillment.

"Destiny is waiting on us." This phrase is fascinating, yet unnerving because destiny is often thought of as something we wait on. But similar to the scientific discovery that light is both particle and a wave; perhaps we too will realize that destiny is both given and received.

IT'S OUR CHOICE

We see an example of this in Genesis 12. God has a destiny waiting for Abram and calls him to leave his life behind and journey to an unknown land. I'm sure he had concerns, but the possibility of life beyond anything ever experienced stood before him. The choice to go is his - and he chooses to take the adventure.

The power to choose… I've met people who thought they had no destiny. I used to believe this about my own life. But the fact we are alive, means there is a destiny waiting for us. We may not know exactly what it is, but it is there - calling our names… And so we must choose whether or not to pursue it.

ARE WE PREPARED?

Only God knows everything. It is impossible to prepare for every situation. Even so, there are seven basic things we must do: 1. Develop our gifts and talents; 2. Learn to think critically about our surroundings; 3. Study our strengths and weaknesses; 4. Build a strong support system of trusted advisors; 5. Routinely learn new things; 6. Guard our emotional, spiritual and physical health; 7. Seek God's guidance in all we do. We must take these steps to journey towards our destiny, while focusing our thoughts in order to establish our purpose.

We must count the cost. Our destiny will always be bigger than us— impacting the lives of others. As fantastic as the sound of destiny is, realize that struggle and obstacles are incorporated into its very fabric. As we press forward we will encounter resistance, because there is an unseen adversary that seeks our destruction. However, God promises to be with us in the midst of our trials, empowering us to learn and overcome. What destiny has God given to you? Will you pursue it or remain comfortable? Remember, that our destiny is as much about the journey as it is about the destination.

As Mark Galli, the author of *Jesus Mean and Wild* states in his book, "God loves you and has a difficult plan for your life." Your Destiny is awaiting your arrival.

ACTION STEPS FOR 2008:

1. Take your Bible to a quiet spot. Read Jeremiah 1:5; 29:11-13; 33:3. Ask God, "What destiny is waiting on me? What am I to do with my life?" Write what comes to you.

2. List your gifts/talents. These can indicate the type of life-work you could be involved in.

3. List your weaknesses and strengths. Perhaps your destiny lies in developing a way to help others deal with similar issues.

4. Revisit those deep dreams that have never left you. Is God trying to call them forth?

5. Determine where you need more development. Pray and brainstorm about how to grow.

6. Follow through… Even with good intentions, no growth or positive change will happen in your life without acting out the plan you have created. Follow Through!

CONCLUSION:

Thank you for taking time to read this book. I hope the content has proven useful as you seek to discover and live out God's dream for your life. Now, the question is, "what do you do next?" Below, you will find ten execution steps to help you MOVE from where you are to a life of greater success and significance.

TOP TEN MOVE STEPS:

1. Pray to God for guidance about your purpose and the strength to change.

2. Ask questions to gain clarity about where you are and where you want to be.

3. Face, acknowledge, and find solutions to remedy your fears and inadequacies.

4. Dream big! Define and write it down. Keep images of your dream before you.

5. Research your dream. Break it into manageable steps with a timeline.

6. Maintain an A.S.K. attitude as you network, network, network.

7. Surround yourself with people who will encourage and challenge you.

8. Discover, develop and display your talents and skills.

9. Exercise your body, mind and spirit, while becoming financially responsible.

10. MOVE on your plan!

PAY IT FORWARD EXERCISE:

Now that you've begun to 'MOVE!' help someone else do the same. This week, choose three people you know and do the following:

A. Ask about their dreams.

B. Help them identify and develop their talents.

C. Speak encouraging words to them.
   (We all deal with negative self-talk.)

D. Help research their dreams.

E. Share opportunities to help get them closer to their dreams.

A CLOSING DECLARATION

The work of living out your destiny may be hard... but in the end it will be well worth it! Focus on your goals. Walk one step at a time. Help others along the way. Take a moment to repeat the personal declaration from the MOVE Manifesto:

"In order for me to MOVE, I must have MOTIVATION: a reason to take the first step forward and every step thereafter. In order for me to MOVE, I need OPTIMISM: an "It's Possible" mindset—otherwise I might as well stay where I am. In order for me to MOVE, I need VISION: the ability to see opportunities in the midst of challenges and difficulties. In order for me to MOVE, I must have ENTHUSIASM: a passion for my journey that beckons others to MOVE in their own lives as well."

Now all you have to do... is MOVE! You can do it!

ALLEN'S READING LIST: BOOKS TO HELP YOU 'MOVE!'

The MI Strategy Bank, DR. ELLEN ARNOLD

The Book of Proverbs, THE HOLY BIBLE

Successful Women Think Differently, VALORIE BURTON

Gifted Hands, DR. BEN CARSON

Take the Risk, DR. BEN CARSON

The Alchemist, PAULO COELHO

The Pact, THE THREE DOCTORS

Financial Peace, DAVE RAMSEY

Life Without Limits, NICK VUJICIC

Speedsuit Powers, ALLEN PAUL WEAVER III

Transition: Breaking Through the Barriers, ALLEN PAUL WEAVER III

The Dream Giver, DAVID WILKINSON

ACKNOWLEDGEMENTS

I want to thank the following people for helping me pull this book together: My wife, Ijnanya for constantly believing in my dreams. Karina, Delores and Frank for reading this manuscript and providing needed constructive criticism. Davina, for providing excellent editorial work. My parents for their encouragement and feedback.

ABOUT THE AUTHOR

For the first half of Allen's life, he just went with the flow of whatever happened. He had no real direction and merely existed. But all of that began to change in college when he discovered several major components of his purpose: written, speech and media communications. A new journey began as he sought to be more intentional about gaining results in his life. Now, 17 years after graduating college, Allen continues to use his gifts and talents to impact others.

As a published author, speaker, workshop facilitator, and filmmaker, Allen Paul Weaver III is dedicated to helping people MOVE from where they are to where they need and want to be. For over a decade, Allen's books, speaking engagements, workshops, and films have helped thousands to:

- Affirm the value of their personal life story.
- Discover their gifts and talents.
- Overcome fears that paralyze daily decision-making.
- Engage in Big Picture seeing & thinking.
- Take calculated risks towards their purpose.
- Transform obstacles into opportunities.
- Pursue their God-given dreams.

Allen is a graduate of Bethune-Cookman University; holding a BA. Degree in Speech/Mass Communications. He is also a graduate of Colgate Rochester Crozer Divinity School; holding an M.Div. Degree in theology.

Allen has published two previous books, **Transition: Breaking Through the Barriers** (2006), an anthology chronicling his journey from adolescence to adulthood; and the young adult novel, **Speedsuit Powers** (2009), which addresses school bullying and has been hailed by readers as an "epic urban adventure story." In 2011, Allen adapted his novel into his first independent feature film, **Speedsuit**. In 2012, a series of private screenings were held to large audiences - receiving critical praise from youth, parents, community leaders, educators and entertainment professionals.

Allen has spoken to large and small audiences at churches and schools and has facilitated workshops at leadership and youth conferences. Allen's message can be summed up as: "Even though we encounter obstacles and fears in life - with God, the right perspective, proper follow-through, and consistency, we can press through and overcome any adversity."

Allen enjoys drawing, producing short films, vertical wind tunnel flying, performing stand-up comedy, innovating new ideas with his brother, and traveling with his wife. He and his wife have one amazing son. To date, he has traveled across the United States, to 7 African countries, China and Europe. He is currently working on several additional book manuscripts for publication.

This can be your year to overcome your fears and pursue your dreams. Let Allen help you MOVE from where you are to where you need and want to be! Read his blog APW3.com, learn more about his books. Invite him to speak at your next event.

DID YOU LIKE THIS BOOK?

Let Allen know: MoveFeedback@allenpaulweaveriii.com

HAVE ALLEN SPEAK AT YOUR NEXT EVENT.

Visit www.allenpaulweaveriii.com to check on availability and pricing.

NOTES

www.ingramcontent.com/pod-product-compliance
Lightning Source LLC
Chambersburg PA
CBHW060421050426
42449CB00009B/2070